Kim Dower's Poetry Is . . .

"Unexpected and sublime."
—O Magazine

"Bold and sexy and smart."
—Stephen Dunn

"Sensual and evocative . . . seamlessly combines humor
and heartache."
—The Los Angeles Times

"A dark chocolate fever dream of love, of mothers. Kim
Dower dares you into the dark. You may find yourself
lurking there."
—Erica Jong

"A kind of miracle . . . wild with poetry's particular fever
. . . but, but, sometimes—tempered by a rich inner life, fed
by wisdom and knowledge one gets walking up and down
upon the earth with all of one's senses fully alert . . . and
this fever can turn into art, as it has, in poem after poem."
—Thomas Lux

"Jazzy, sassy, sexy—poems that move fast, are full of
surprise and tweak the heartstrings like Arkhipovsky
tweaks the balalaika."
—Stephen Dobyns

LAST TRAIN TO THE
Missing Planet

poems

KIM DOWER

RED HEN PRESS | *Pasadena, CA*

Book design by Marcia Langren

Library of Congress Cataloging-in-Publication Data

Names: Dower, Kim, author.
Title: Last train to the missing planet / Kim Dower.
Description: Pasadena : Red Hen Press, 2016.
Identifiers: LCCN 2015046506 | ISBN 9781597093538 (softcover)
Subjects: | BISAC: POETRY / American / General.
Classification: LCC PS3604.O9395 A6 2016 | DDC 811/.6—dc23
LC record available at http://lccn.loc.gov/2015046506

The Los Angeles County Arts Commission, the National Endowment for the Arts, the Pasadena Arts & Culture Commission and the City of Pasadena Cultural Affairs Division, Sony Pictures Entertainment, the Los Angeles Department of Cultural Affairs, the Dwight Stuart Youth Fund, and Ahmanson Foundation partially support Red Hen Press.

First Edition
Published by Red Hen Press
www.redhen.org

Acknowledgments

Many thanks to the editors of the following journals and publications in which these poems first appeared: *Arroyo Monthly*: "Eating Yogurt with a Knife," "13 Knishes," "Scrambling Eggs," "My Mother Bakes Sugar Cookies," and "While Waiting on the Food Truck Line"; *Barrow Street*: "Lipstick Reading"; *Coiled Serpent: Poets Arising from the Cultural Quakes & Shifts in Los Angeles* (Tia Cucha Press, 2016): "Fontanel" and "Workout"; *Connotation Press—An Online Artifact*: "I could sleep for days on a bed of lapels," "Home Invasion," and "My Mailman Pees on the Gate by the Dumpster"; *Life and Legend*: "My Guardian" and "A Fly with One Wing is Watching Me"; *The Los Angeles Review*: "Fontanel" and "How to Celebrate the End of the World"; *Rattle*: "I wore this dress today for you, mom."

I am forever grateful to Terry Wolverton, my poem whisperer, and to the insightful and talented poets at "Writers at Work;" to Erica Jong for her wisdom and inspiration; to Thomas Lux, the Master, for getting me hooked so many years ago; to the amazing poets at the Palm Beach Poetry Festival, including Gregory Orr, Laura Kasischke, and Robert Wrigley, whose invaluable teachings helped to inform some of the poems in this book; to my beloved friends and devoted readers, Janice Holden and Debra Ollivier, for telling me the truth; to my son, Max, who often comes up with the perfect word; to Kate Gale and Mark E. Cull—extraordinary, creative, multi-talented, ceaselessly energetic, gifted publishers of Red Hen Press—for believing in these poems and for publishing so many wonderful writers who continue to astonish.

Lastly, to my Poetry Angel—wing to wing—forever.

For Thom

CONTENTS

[II]

[III]

[IV]

[V]

[VI]

[VII]

I'm wearying to escape into that glorious world, and to be always there: not seeing it dimly through tears, and yearning for it through the walls of an aching heart: but really with it, and in it.

—Emily Brontë

LAST TRAIN TO THE MISSING PLANET

How to Celebrate the End of the World

Undress.
Take everything off. Everything.
Rub your nipples with grape seed oil.
Sit up straight in your most uncomfortable chair.
Remind yourself of all the good things you've done.
Have you done anything good?
Tell me what you've done.
Have you given birth to a child
Who danced around the house wearing a ninja costume?
Did you visit your dying mother every last day until
The day she died whispering thank you inside your moist hands?
Be quiet.
Don't look me in the eyes. Look down.
Have you cooked meals for the homeless?
Sat with them while they ate?
Have you ever rescued anyone?
Tell me the good things you've done.
Then remember the times you lost yourself in sorrow.
Waded in pools of it, banged your head against the ledge,
Hated yourself for wanting love, or showing how you felt.
Remember the moments it hurt so bad you had to pull out
Just in time. Let's prepare together for the end of the world.
Forget what I previously said. Let's dress. Let's layer ourselves
With color, texture, linen and cashmere, beads in our hair, smear
Our blood on one another's faces. Stretch ourselves
Into eternity, breathe life into whatever dream we've been keeping
Under wraps, jump the fence together, melt the line with heat
From our kisses, obliterate it with desire, cross over
Into the end of the world, the beginning of another, locked
In an emergency embrace.

[I]

ANOTHER MORNING

Dawn cracks me open like a clam
light and salt dissolve my dream
as daylight stretches over me
its hands reaching for the last

moments of darkness.
Your chest radiates heat
against my back, a snap of cold
hits my legs where the blanket

has fallen. I feel your breath
on my neck, your teeth behind me
or are those my teeth? Am I alone
pretending it's you pushing me

out of sleep, or us together,
a team half waking? Let's stay
in our shell, you say, or did I
say that as I step onto

my morning escalator *all aboard*
to the top floor, the sky, the birds
the billow clouds they'll all be there
on this fine spring day—orange

blossoms—can you smell them too
we'll smell them together, we'll pick
some buds, no you'll pick them
and give them to me, oh

the slanted day! how the fog lifts
after it's wrapped me like silk
weaved me through all the yous
I've ever let inside the curtain

where the echo is uncertain, here
where my arms gather us in a cocoon,
where it's just me taking us on another
morning walk under the tired moon.

Only You Are You

The way your lips curve
into a half way smile
like the joke's not ready

you save the punch
line for dark.
Only you are the tiger

in my recurring dream
giant cat I taunt, run from.
Only you are the one I speak to

when I'm not speaking,
blanket that covers me
wraps me tight until dawn

as you hike the shadowed hills,
moon stepping back just for you
only you, offering a fresh sky.

I'll never know where you go,
wish I could rescue you
make us real make us right,

woo you out from the cave
where your heart hides you,
bare, unfed, not able to dig

into the lighthouse of bones
we both crave to suck dry.
I sleep inside your mouth,

echo of your voice vibrates
like music from a party
in a far away room;

can you hear it, too, only you?

SELF-PORTRAIT WITH IMAGINARY BROTHER

after de Kooning

My imaginary brother is not made of charcoal and ink,
living on paper. He is made of ashes and dust, particles of light
breathing down through the night.

Gone before he was ever born, I've only heard about him
how he would have been the first, miscarried by my mother.
He was too young to care, but I know

he exists out there in the air because sometimes I feel a kiss
but no one's there. I want to believe that if he'd been born,
he'd have pulled me in a wagon

through the park in a storm. He'd have guarded my room
wearing shields and armor, helped the rest of us learn to be calmer.
I wonder does my mother

ever think of him now—her first she never had?
And, though she has me and my other brother, would she have
loved him more, and would I

have looked more like the other, my imaginary brother,
the one who'd have taught me to swim through the ocean in a storm?
In my self-portrait with imaginary brother,

we sit in a field facing one another.
Painted in bright colors, oil and acrylic on board,
my hair is pink, my lips are black; we each hold a sword.

Lunar Eclipse

Late tonight when the moon passes
behind the earth, you will be high

in the canyon, at home with your solitude,
owls and coyotes, the city as far below

as the stars are miles above,
while I will be in the black speckled sky

dancing between two nameless stars
waiting to see the moon kissed

by the earth's shadow, waiting for you
to come find me so we can watch

as it slowly creeps across, slips away.
You will come right at the moment

the moon bursts into orange, turns red.
We will feast on blood in the sky.

Theft

Earth stole its moon
from Venus

as you have stolen
my heart from me

You hold it in your hands
a red bird throbbing

You put it in the nest
of your twigged soul

feel its song melt
through your body

Earth stole its moon
from Venus

as you have stolen
my heart from me

with skillful hands
not afraid

of the ecstatic glow
burning your fingers

BACK THEN

All of us swam out
past the raft
that rocked steadily
looked so small
until we circled back
we'd all pack on top
like bodies in a grave
still breathing
wet with salt
our legs one over the other
your hand on my belly
we didn't cry back then
just lived
like it didn't matter
like sadness wasn't
born yet.

What She Wants

She wants to take the rocks
out of his pockets
be the puzzle
he keeps going back to
the clue
that solves it
she wants to be the sweat
on his neck
his holiday dinner
with two kinds of stuffing
the bandage across his chest
that stops the bleeding
the wax he drips
on his other
girlfriend's belly
the breeze
through his window
the butter he licks
from the corners
of his mouth
the only kiss
lingering on his lips
the milk in his coffee
the recurring dream
he waits for
book he gets lost in
kitten he rescues from the alley
she wants to be his last
meal before they flip
the switch and she wants to be

the one that pulls him
out of the chair
the shoes he wears
to escape
the song he sings
as they're running

Half Way Home

pink Virgin tube in the air
strapped in my seat
red wine tv screen all i can eat
playing with words
stringing them together
flying home where i want to be
where my lemon tree waits
for me suck its tartness
new york miles away
way down there new york i no longer know
clean safe not where i grew up
not for me anymore i long for
what will never be mine
dangerous shadows los angeles colors
my heart promises to be uncovered
long for my bed
the moments undiscovered
my plane eating out the darkness
swallowing the sky sucking up stars
that get in its way
no moon tonight just birds their feathers parted
sleeping between constellations
the ocean waiting for my arrival rolling over
secrets it covers folded into waves
uncovers i want to be home i want to be making
another world starving for the finish line
landing pulling back where is my home
where will you find me

THE RACCOON ON WILLOUGHBY

I'm in the city of L.A., on Willoughby,
traffic, hamburgers flipping, bellybuttons
pierced on every corner, a raccoon
wanders out of a stranger's yard,
braided eyes, dark mask like in books,
his tail like Davy Crockett's cap.
He acts guilty like he knows something,
looks behind him as he claws up the fence.
We make eye contact, I'm still
in my car afraid to get out, afraid he might
bite spit rush lunge, give me rabies.
He's a super raccoon in a super town,
alone on a raccoon mission, or a drifting
waiter, ex-actor, a genie turned into a raccoon,
cursed, searching for a prince or princess to kiss,
make him human again I stay in my car
watch him from my rear view mirror as he gets
smaller and smaller, scrambles his way down
the broken raccoon sidewalk to find the one
who can break the spell. It could have been me.

As long as my mother keeps getting mail

she's not really dead. Pink Dot Free Delivery,
Appleseed's catalogue, The Democratic Party—
when something arrives for her in my box,
which is where her mail's been forwarded,
I open it, read it to her, so she knows
people still care. Better insurance,
a chance to cast her vote. It still happens
without her. As long as my mother
keeps getting mail she is still alive!
I reinstate her membership to AARP
so they will send a free insulated tote bag,
which I will keep for me. Even alive
she'd never have used it. She'll never know
I stole it. She won't be mad because she's dead.
Today her new Discover Card was delivered along
with a letter from her secret love. Who's to say
the dead can't continue to enjoy their lives?

Desire is the Fire

It isn't always what you have
Fills your life with pleasure
Often what you wish was yours
Becomes your secret treasure

[II]

I WORE THIS DRESS TODAY FOR YOU, MOM,

breezy floral, dancing with color
soft, silky, flows as I walk.
Easter Sunday and you always liked

to get dressed, go for brunch, "maybe
there's a good movie playing somewhere?"
Wrong religion, we were not church-goers,

but New Yorkers who understood the value
of a parade down 5ᵗʰ Avenue, bonnets
in lavender, powder blues, pinks, hues

of spring, the hope it would bring.
We had no religion but we did have
noodle kugel, grandparents, dads

who could fix fans, reach the china
on the top shelf, carve the turkey.
That time has passed. You were the last

to go, mom, and I still feel bad I never
got dressed up for you like you wanted me to.
I had things, things to do. But today in L.A.

hot the way you liked it—those little birds
you loved to see flitting from tree to tree—
just saw one, a twig in its mouth, preparing

a bed for its baby—might still be an egg,
I wish you were here. I've got a closet filled
with dresses I need to show you.

"Visiting Eleanor"

Barbara, my childhood piano teacher
played Chopin like he was whispering
into her hands, all us kids from the building
had our Saturday morning lessons, apartment 6C,
our giddy fingers trotting in the key of G,
lifting high for Mozart, metronome ticking
as her coffee brewed, her sandy-haired husband
at the wooden breakfast table, mug, cigarette
tight in his hands, he was the man on the Winston
ads, I'd slide by him, eyes down on my way
to the bedroom where the shining black upright
Steinway sat facing Broadway, her daughter pirouetting
across the checkered linoleum floor, tiny yellow socks
collecting dust with each step, twirling to the music
we were all struggling so hard to learn how to play.
And here we are a lifetime later, arm in arm, walking
in the rain, joyous as a sonata on our way to 72nd street,
"visiting Eleanor," she calls it "the only statue of a woman
in the entire city," tightening her grip, her bicep strong
as a ballerina's calf muscle, and it all comes back,
she and my mother close talking in our kitchen, Barbara's pink
mohair sweater, hair in rollers, the two of them always
wanting to put things behind them, the music of their motherhood,
beat of secrets, music of being someone's daughter. I still have
my music book filled with her notes: "moderate tempo, allegro,
practice! *Here's* where you get into trouble."

SLEEP OVER

The sound of water screeching to a boil
reminds me of my grandmother's
trembling hand pouring her steam-hissing

kettle over the Lipton's teabag settled
in her white porcelain cup.
Those would be the mornings I'd have slept over

on the pull out in the living room, bundled in flannel,
watching lights from traffic below make angels on the ceiling.
My grandfather would already be out for the day,

picking up a nice brisket, a few carrots, nodding
to shopkeepers on his walk down Broadway, picking
the wrong horses at the corner OTB. He'd only bet ponies

with the same name as one of his daughters, or grandchildren,
a horse with a name that started with "K" or "J," "S" or "N."
In the evening I'd watch grownups as if studying another species:

Gretel with her bargains, "I got this sweater for 99 cents!"
Catherine the milliner, hat pins sticking out of the sides of her mouth.
Why did my grandmother hide money in a drawer

under the kitchen table? How was she able
to put her red lipstick on without a mirror, never going
out of the lines? Who was Uncle Joe? Why'd she shriek

at my grandfather when he returned from the store
without the dill after dark because he'd forgotten his way home?
Why did he never say anything back, but just look at me

sitting at the fold out card table where I'd been waiting all day to watch him
rip the cellophane off a new Bicycle deck, break it open, shuffle, "let's play,"
I've got a hand like a foot," he'd always say.

You are waking in the city where I was born

As the sun rises over Manhattan
it's still dark out here, jasmine wafting
through my window, heat wave in April,
Santa Ana winds lifting bones from the earth
lifting me out of sleep thinking of you waking
to the sounds of chilly city life your hotel robe
your only warmth. I want to be there with you,
get you a buttered kaiser from Deluca's Market,
coffee with extra cream, take you to see
the horse and buggies by the entrance of the park,
feed the ducks, sure there are ducks in New York
near the Carousel where we'd get stoned between classes,
back then when the city wasn't for winners, just a place to grow,
get fucked up, listen to our parents' jazz records
while we snuck off to sounds of our own—
Max's Kansas City wearing black eyeliner, dresses up
our asses, taking chances, cutting classes, my grandmother
pulling another capon out of the oven while
my grandfather tossed back his second vodka proud
he was a pharmacist at Charles Chemist on Broadway
where I'd go pocket a lipstick—new shade—hi, grandpa
no one was looking, life was easier when we took the bus
had turkey on rye, Russian dressing, cole slaw on the sandwich,
and there you are waking to the dissonant sounds
of Grand Central Station, rain staining your 39th floor window,
people moving fast down below, they all have someplace,
someplace to go, it's still New York things must get done,
the cabbies are changing shifts and you are waking
to the bliss of my past, hiss of a million radiators, warming the night.
Head to Madison, see the shops, the long-legged women smoking

as they flock cross town, peek into places no one will tell you about, streets you'll find on your own, but please go to St. Patrick's Cathedral light candles for the dead, if you do one thing do that, I wish I was with you to show you what no longer exists, what used to be, right there where you're standing—right there where you're making history.

There will be things you do

you won't know why.
Maybe waiting to tie
your shoelaces

until everything else
is in place.
Could be you'll slide

your egg yolks aside
eat every bit of bacon,
toast, whites while the forsaken

yellow orbs stare at you
from the side pocket
of your empty plate.

People will ask
why do you save
your yolks for last

and you won't know—
won't recall
the cousin from the south

came to visit one summer
ate his eggs so odd
your family said

stuck with you
like the way
you love to be kissed

on the back of your neck
can vaguely recollect
your mother's kisses

after your bath
too gentle for memory.
There will be things you do

you won't know why
like the way you look
up at the sky

when anxious or blue
it's what your father
used to do

every family trip
when nothing else
was right

except those clouds
moving north by northwest
through the night

he showed you
what pilots knew:
factors for safe flying

are visibility
and how low
and mean the clouds are.

How I Learned to Love

By trusting the moon even when I couldn't see it
By watching my cat lick between her claws

By watching them kiss in *Splendor in the Grass*
I leaned over the couch so I could see up close
No space between them so their love
Could not escape

I never meant to leave the milk out
Didn't want to be late for the game
I learned to love by feeling bad, feeling shame

I learned to love by protecting everyone but me
A spider edging along the window sill

13 Knishes

A friend brings me 13 knishes
from Brighton Beach
carries them in a plastic bag
on the airplane from New York
to L.A.: potato, meat, kasha
I didn't know *what* to say. I'm touched
he thought of me, wanted
to surprise me, the weight alone
daunting, carrying onto the plane
even if it crashed he'd have
held them tight, gone down
the emergency slide clutching them,
those knishes brought me back
so many memories riding the D
from Manhattan to the beach
I was a teen, towel rolled under my arm
would stop at that dive under the "EL"
eat one before I hit the sand
like a punch in the stomach
even without gravy that knish
was lethal, and now I have 13.
How could he know the smell
alone set me back remembering the man
standing over me, blocking the sun
not a soul on the sand, my eyes closed
body slathered in Coppertone
he bent down, kissed me on the lips
said, *that's what we do where I come from,*
I said, this is America, I'm 16, just want a tan,
and I could never shake that dread

like a knish in my stomach feeling
like lead, a gift from a place long ago
way before I knew how to say no.

Years later,

sitting in my backyard
relieved to be feeling whole
with only a breeze for conversation
I think about you and how you loved
water sports, diving into the murky lake
while I'd hang on the beach zipped up
in a life preserver, promising I might
go on the boat for a quick ride around the edge
of the shore. I asked you to never turn on
the motor when I was aboard, *I like to take it slow,*
I told you, *take in the scenery.*
Once you brought a picnic:
lopsided sandwiches, meat half off,
not sure where you found the bread
but I forced mine down with a gulp
of Pabst, (made your nuts cousin buy it for us),
iced cold and tasting nasty.
I would have done anything with you
back then, when the moon was watching
only us, your golden eyes, super hero
shoulders, would have split my life in two
with the paddle from your canoe would have
let you cut me deepest, but what was the use?
I was a summer visitor in your year round world
too young to know why it was okay.
Your hair smelled of cedar, was held back
with a clip belonging to your winter girlfriend.
You were mine for July and I was terrified
of the shortness of the ride.

GOODBYE TO JAMES GARNER

Fans loved him as *Rockford, Maverick,*
a man's man, had your back, cool,
did the right thing. I loved him
for being Doris Day's husband
in a movie I cut class to see,
fifth grade, played at the Riviera,
only old men and me during the day,
went alone told no one, but I had a gigantic
crush, he was an ob/gyn, she was a mom,
marriage in jeopardy, couples in movies
stayed together in the sixties, while out
in the world it was all falling apart, women
poised to flip their lives, marching into a world
of miniskirts, riots, shame, pill box hats, flinging
our boxy pink suit jackets and pumps into the sunset,
not even James Garner could have saved us, and this week
more unrest, more wars, I'm stuck on the headline
James Garner Dead. When I was ten I needed a man
I could count on—even a man holding aces and eights.

THE FRENCH WOMAN DOCTOR IN MY DREAM

The French women doctor in my dream
tall and slender, long dark braid down her back
loved you like I never could. You were stricken
by her elegance, let her heal you in places
I didn't know were ailing. Your right shoulder,
for example, she knew it was tight, needed rotating
so she shook you hard. I could hear your muscles
cry out beneath your skin. I was jealous watching her
manipulate you, how you were paralyzed by her touch
this slender French woman with a braid down her back,
just like my grandmother's braid who you never knew,
never even knew I had a grandmother. She was so strong,
capable, petite in her little cape that swung from her shoulders,
Russian accent, you would have liked that too, you,
always searching for a cure, an adjustment, two fine hands
to put you in your place as the dust settles around us,
sun heating our skin, my dream bursting the truth right out of me

SCRAMBLING EGGS

When you scramble eggs,
I show my daughter as I pour
the raw liquid onto the readied pan,
it doesn't matter whether you go slow
gently fold them into the heat
or snap your wrist—flip them over
faster than the flame
the taste of the eggs,
the memory of having eaten them,
will be the same. I don't have
a daughter, but this morning
when scrambling my eggs
deliberately, not hurriedly
as I usually do, I thought
if I had a daughter
this is what I'd tell her.
I'd wait until she was seven
and remind her again at twenty-one.

Easter Sunday

She'd always wished
this could *really* be her holiday

colored eggs, a basket of jelly beans
floating on fake grass, pastel ribbons

her mother laid out on her bed
(there'd be a soft bunny, too,

bright ears, black beads for eyes),
but where was the magical gold cross?

Jesus didn't belong to her
like he belonged to the ladies in mint

green coats, pouring into
St. Patrick's Cathedral hemorrhaging

rebirth, while she'd be at Tip Toe Inn
spreading Russian dressing

on her lean corned beef, her grandmother
in elbow length gloves, winter chill still

in the New York air, pretending she was in Church
like Donna and her sisters, praying to be forgiven.

[III]

MOTHER'S DAY

They all climb into her bed bringing breakfast lunch and dinner.
All her children, her friends with children, their children,
her mother, her mother's mother, the daughters she never had,
the ones with long hair she never spent hours braiding.

They are all naked except for scarves which they wear on their heads
or covering their shoulders, or tied around their waists.
It's Mother's Day and they're ready to celebrate.
Who's hungry, her mother asks all the mothers and their children?

We are all hungry, they say, as they grab the hardboiled eggs
jiggling in a blue ceramic bowl in the middle of the bed. *We are all
thirsty, too*, say the little ones, holding up their sippy cups,
their scarves sliding off their heads, their mothers ferociously

Tying knots that won't slip under their chins. Her mother's mother
is so old she doesn't know it's Mother's Day. She doesn't ever remember
not being a mother, has sweet butter in her veins, has made so many
beds she doesn't know why she's in this one. *Who are all these people,*

She asks one of the unknown children. *I don't know*, says the little boy.
*I don't want my scarf. I left my robot in my room and I forgot to turn him off.
He's probably left the house, on his way to the park or maybe back to Jupiter, or
getting ice cream. My mother is taking too long and I want to go home.*

Lunch with Gloria

First we compare sweaters: rayon, cashmere,
agree we only want to wear what's super soft,

no more itchy for us, ever. She tells me
she loves linen but I say, no! Too scratchy,

stiff, unyielding. If linen could talk it would say things
that hurt. *You just have to know how to care for linen,*

Gloria tells me, inviting me to touch her blouse.
Feel how soft. It wrinkles terribly, but I don't care:

it's a fabric of special qualities—complex, rare
one can hardly complain when it knots up.

We talk necklaces, how we want ours to tell stories
about the people who gave them to us, which occasions.

She shows me hers—a ring on a chain from a young man
she'll always love. He's gone now but never gone

from her heart. I show her the locket hiding behind my shirt.
I got this for myself after my son was born, rose gold,

tiny ruby, just one eye peeking out of the stroller,
my baby's face, the size of a sigh.

Fontanel

He's so lucky
the brain doctors
tell me, huddled in white
their names embroidered

in blue script across
their chests, my grown son
sprawled across the hospital bed
tubes, needles sticking

into his body, twined
around him like veins
through a parched leaf.
I can't look at him

his mouth crusted
unfocused eyes
that yesterday lit up
the room, now his skull

fractured, same head
I used to hold in one hand
his legs rocking my arm
to sleep. Infant's heads

are so soft, easy
to rupture, brains still
forming. I can't look at him now
his giant hands, filth baked

under his nails
from scratching the gutter
where he fell off
the back of a car—

of course he shouldn't have
been sitting on the trunk
of a car—but you see
they will do things

they will do things
that can hurt and we have to watch
and when I see him in that bed
hooked up to machines beeping

instructions to the nurse
making noise like garbage trucks
on collection day
I have to look away

cover my eyes like he did
when he was three
afraid to see
the flying monkeys

in the Wizard of Oz,
he'd run screaming
into my lap. Where is it now
The Emerald City?

Where can I get the courage
to uncover my eyes
see the blood
ooze from his ear

walk over to the bed
whisper, *I'm here, it'll be ok*
you're lucky, the doctors say
but all I can think

is what if it hadn't
gone this way—
luck, the slippery slope
of miracles, unpredictable

fragile as a fontanel
soft luck running out
from the moment
we're born.

PREGNANT

In my dream last night I whispered in Meryl Streep's ear
that I was pregnant. "That's great," she said, her eyes
searching my face, but "I'm 60," I whispered. "Oh my,"
she said, touching my cheek, asking who the father was
my husband, I told her, thank god, she said, but we parted
uncomfortably, me not even knowing her well in the first place,
so I had hoped to make a good impression. When I met the doctor
I was unsure how I felt, would he be able to handle this kind of
older pregnancy, what kind of mother to a tween would I be at
70, would I still be doing car pool in my golden years, choosing
prom dresses from catalogs side by side with my medical
equipment journals, the horrors of old age juxtaposed with
cheerful youth seemed insurmountable and so I consulted
my best friend Janice, she was very blonde in my dream with
peach complexion, turquoise earrings, looked like a sweet
nursery school teacher, she was concerned but steady,
asked me if I'd consider an abortion and I burst into tears,
the hot kind that burn as they roll down and if skin on your
face is already chapped from cold days of long walks those
tears are truly unpleasant, so we didn't say the word abortion
again not that I have a moral problem with it, but if there's life
inside me I want to see what kind of life it is, I want to hold it
at the end of that long day, I want to make it grilled cheese,
swing it into the sky on a beach day, I want to read it *Where's Waldo*

HOME INVASION

Driving while sipping a mixture of peach nectar, bee pollen,
coconut water, breaking news on the car radio: home invasion
Highland and Melrose, they've broken into a board and care,
elderly people in chairs, squad cars circling, helicopter above.
The black cat with no name who hangs around my house,
tags that say, "I am an outside cat," and "I know my way home,"
came inside yesterday. I had left the door open so my blind,
deaf dog could let himself out, and the cat slithered in,
made himself comfortable, rolled around on my crushed
velvet couch, his silver tags clinking. My dog knew something
was up, sniffed around but couldn't find the cat , so cool, jumping
over the pillows onto the coffee table, burying his nose into my roses,
my dog, who spends his days sleeping, went nuts trying to find him,
caught the scent, was revived, sprung into action with athletic timing,
lunged, bit him on the ass—this cat never saw it coming—ran out
the opened door, my dog all proud, macho having protected his home,
and as I slurp the last bit of juice—color of bile—bee pollen filling
my stomach, firing up my brain, I turn up the radio, they've got
the perps outside the house on Highland, hands behind their backs,
folks inside board and care alert, nodding their heads, trading
excitement. *I knew something was up,* says a man whose family
hasn't heard him speak for months.

We Took Off in the Snow

Flew up into white air everywhere
white into grey smoke through the bright
curtain of sun streaming down
through the cold meeting blue
We're safe now the snow
falls only below
Up here we no longer care
My toddler son sucks
his yellow plastic butterfly
seatbelt tight as the plane
reaches cruising I sip vodka on ice
lick salt from my fingers greasy from nuts
This is a family trip
My husband sits further back
seat 32A I turn to give him the "ok,"
we're fine up here more steady
than we are on the ground
where life changes as fast as our son's moods
where we don't believe in heaven
not like up here where I just
saw it peek through
mountains of dunes drifting like snow
remember the snow
on the ground when we left
when you're high enough
35,000 feet new clouds will break apart
opening to a different heaven you can view
the world differently even a river
might appear as your son sleeps
your husband way in back

will close his eyes and his head will tip
touching the woman's arm next to him
she herself asleep dreaming
of the man she hasn't yet met
who'll kiss her as the clouds part
snow falling below plane cruising
my boy's lips stuck to the butterfly as I
remember long ago sitting alone in my room
listening to the traffic below waiting
to be older so I could fly away

BLUE SHEETS

Ever since I've been sleeping
on the new blue sheets
I've been having nightmares.
I don't blame the sheets
or you for having bought them,
I can only blame my subconscious,
waiting like a kidnapper to lure me
inside another epic dream, my
subconscious—slave to the drudge
it collects, sweeps into corners of my brain—
rusty nails, screams, broken glass—
exploding bushels of dryer lint bursting
from windows, oozing from rooms
I never knew we had, lint from every
wash I've ever done, choking grey
lint so fierce it makes the house
rumble, floor boards loosening like gigantic
molars, as my face embraces the softness
of the sheets, as you sleep by my side,
my house, our house, comes apart,
blue sheets beneath me hugging
the mattress—my raft, horse, train, guide—
carrying me beyond the hours of night,
until the black sky dissolves into the first
ache of morning, your eyes still closed.

Minor Tremors

Family photos slanted
on the wall
must have shifted
after a small quake
I never felt
the impact of
I only remember that big one
shaking us awake at 4am
the two of us
trying to balance our way
along rippling floorboards
palms flat against the wall
our bodies hurled
down the long hall
struggling against the obscene
force of earth
to retrieve our son
sleeping in his crib

Can't put my finger on
the years
of minor tremors
between then and now
but I know things have changed
When did the cup on the top shelf
topple to its side
when did the hairline
fracture on the living room wall
become a crack spreading across the ceiling
When did I feel the shift

in my heart
They say the small ones
relieve the pressure
so the big one won't come
Still, every time I feel a truck
rumble through the alley
I brace myself
for the ground to finally open
I'm ready to slip away
into its burning core

She can't hear the things he says,

yet she listens anyway
knowing his words will cut her
like shards of glass from a flask

in which she'd like to mix him
a special cocktail.

She no longer feels sick
when his rants slice her in half
chooses to believe

he doesn't realize what he's saying,
how it sounds.

He'd better not touch her,
better not reach across the 400 thread count
pima cotton rose colored sheets crisscrossed
with blush stripes—*subtle* he said

when she brought them home,
they blend into the fabric, fade into the pattern
like a frightened child fades into the back

of her closet,
hides from the screamers

protected by darkness, holds her own hand.

They can't get me here, she thinks,

but here she is again,
grown up, in the back of a different closet,

threadbare ribbon laced around her soul
coming undone,

she's trying to power through the tunnel of un-love,
gathering the strong ones still alive inside her.

NATURAL DISASTERS

After a natural disaster, limbs under cars,
people floating on rafts through city streets
with nothing but their wounded pets,
life changing decisions will be made:
do we embrace what remains—
hold tight to those we thought we loved,
have tried to love, or do we finally
cut lose, free ourselves of lives unreal,
exfoliate ourselves from ourselves,
remove each dead layer of life,
give ourselves the other chance we never
thought we'd have?
What kinds of disasters lead to disasters
of the heart, the ones that take place over years,
like marinating a cow, still alive, uncut, basted
day after day until all liquids are absorbed,
engorged into flesh, bone, tendons, until
too succulent to eat.
The soggy remains of love.
Crumbling fireplace bricks after the big one,
pieces of cement, clay under your fingernails,
dusting particles off your coat forever.
Spelling H E L P with your underwear on the tree outside
your house, protective head gear at dinner.
For some of us it takes an earthquake to be set free.
For others a tsunami—years of disaster brewing
under the sea only to swell up when you're already
gone. Love, like the ocean floor, is varied and irregular
and like the land it will never die. It can be destroyed
with one word uttered same as a jolt

through the earth, or can fade after years
of anemia, two dispirited souls rubbing
against each other in sleep, evaporating
like milk on a hot sidewalk, and like all natural disasters,
it's only a cleansing for the paradise that can lie ahead.

PUNCH MASSAGE

This is what they do
to relieve the pain.

Stay still, he says, as he thrusts
his fist into her belly

turning the color of a child's
cocktail, not quite pink,

rosy as her cheek
when fever would spike.

Don't move, he says, as he jabs
his knuckles into her gut.

She keeps her eyes open,
do it harder, she whispers,

her voice hoarse with
expectations, and he delivers

his face, neck coated with sweat
another fast one in her sweet spot

where they cut the cord
when she was born,

the core from where she needs
to be released once more

so she can enter his rage
pavilion, live inside his anger,

disappear in the glow, the power
of his hands. He wants to be sure

she can take all he's got to give,
hopes she asks him for more.

This is how they create. This is how
they know who they are.

TELL ME

for Baudelaire

Tell me, mysterious stranger,
whom do you love the best:
your mother, your wife
your daughter or your lover?

I have neither wife, nor daughter
my mother has passed,
my lover has vanished. I have only
the vague scent of her perfume
infused in my skin.

Your country?
I cannot love what I do not trust.

Your friends?
Friends are for the young.

Then tell me, whom do you love?

I love the moon
the moon that changes
with the whims
of the earth. I love
how it pulls me
to where I will never reach
how the stars
cry out for its attention
protect its glaring pain

I love the moon
how it empties its shine
into morning

[**IV**]

Day Whatever of Heat Wave

I awaken again
predawn heat clawing the walls
dead air folding me over
like a drunk lover
my body has absorbed
this heat that my useless fan
has churned through the night
my chest moist back of my neck
wet like when I was sick as a child
they had to lower me
into a tub filled with ice
I'm too tired to feed my dog
who can't make it to his water dish
even the birds on my lemon tree
don't dare move, conserving their energy
getting ready to fly out of town
Alaska, I heard one of them say,
it's cold there let's go just for fun
I want cold my legs are heavy
my arms useless weights
I cannot lift the toast to my lips
soon this, too, will be a memory
the jacket in my closet waits for its moment
taunts me with its fleece and corduroy
soon enough I'll be shivering
on some street corner
wishing for a heat filled night
when being naked was my only option

It's Wednesday, Not Thursday

Wake up thinking it's trash day
so I move the cans out to the front
even though it's pouring. Back in,
make extra strong coffee,
read the story in the paper
about the 400-pound bear they
captured in La Crescenta, he strolled down
the mountain, lured by the scent
of meatballs from Costco,
made several trips sensing the danger
but those of us who've had them can agree
those meatballs from Costco are worth
getting pierced by tranquilizer darts.
"Like moving a water bed without a frame,"
claimed the State Fish and Game officials
who loaded him into the truck.
I hope a princess kisses him, he wakes up
human, marries, lives happily ever after
in a home at the edge of a forest
where a bear will stray from the mountain,
raid his garbage, and the ex-bear, father of two,
will keep buckets of chilled meatballs in every room
of his sprawling ranch-style home.

I Want to See You Glow,

he tells me, so I rub pet products
over my body, oil to make a dog's coat
glossy. The hair on my arms is sparse,
but I run fast and have an appetite
like a Weimaraner. I want to feel
as good to the touch as a dog
after a day in a dog spa, as energetic,
intelligent, alert, steady. This human
life is not right anymore. Look around.
Join me for a chew treat and a dish of water.

SMALL WAISTS, BIG BUTTS

The Style Section says small waists and big butts
are "in" this year. This is good news for many women—
Arlene, for example, my counselor from Camp Trywoodie,
bunk 10, she comes to mind, had a stomach flat as a bench press,
but no bathing suit could ever cover that butt of hers,
and we'd all try to catch a glimpse as she pulled
the red and black spandex over her thighs, her ass, just so,
primping to sunbathe by the lake while we'd all be jumping
off rowboats, drowning, she'd be greasing up that tight belly of hers
for Buddy, in charge of all dock activities, Buddy, who was always
carrying the oars. Where is Arlene now? I want to tell her
The New York Times reports the world is ready to embrace her shape,
accept her, no—want her just as she is, no need to keep running in place,
no more wild horseback riding, knocking her butt against the wall,
no more cellulite injections, flirting with liposuction.
The article says women are actually padding their underwear
to get that full, rounded look, padding their underwear, my God,
I spent my high school years feeling myself up to make sure mine
wasn't spreading, and Arlene, who knows? Someone please get on Facebook,
there must be a way to find her, tell her the news that she can shimmy
in and out of any room knowing everyone's watching with envy, lust,
craves a pinch, a touch, a swing like that in their backyard.

LEADER OF THE PRETTY GIRL PARTY

The man with one eye yells to me
here comes the leader of the pretty girl party
and I find it hard to breathe.

He doesn't wear a patch so I can see
his bum eye is closed for life like a mouth
sewn shut, the other clear blue watches

as I walk up the street. He's camped on a plastic
lawn chair outside a storefront boxing ring
heckling me with kindness.

I won't look into his good eye
as he tracks my steps. *Here she comes—the leader
of the pretty girl party*, but now he's yelling

to someone else. I just want to get to my car
struggle to remember where it's parked, self-
conscious, angry at flowers, angry

at the Craftsman houses. A mangy white dog
lays by his feet, licks his toes.
Doesn't he mean pretty girl *club*, because party

doesn't make any sense. I see my car in the distance.
Sudden chill as a ribbon of cloud covers the sun.
Nobody can see the air as it dresses to get ready for evening.

Eating Yogurt with a Knife

This morning I ate my yogurt with a knife
which is not as hard as you may think

a black plastic knife, easy to slide
into my mouth and the yogurt seemed to glide

with an ease I've never experienced.
You taste it differently, not in one lump

but rather your mouth has a chance
to get used to the yogurt being slipped in.

Unless one is forced into a situation where one
is starving, there's no spoon, you'll do whatever

it takes to get that yogurt into your body, even rip
the damn thing open and drink it, one will never

discover the wonders of eating yogurt with a knife.
Try it. Not when you're desperate, but when

it's your choice. Do it because you want to.
Do it because you can.

Time of Arrival

I called my mother last night
to tell her my plane had landed,
I'd be home for dinner, but she
wasn't there. She was there,
like on the phone, but she wasn't
there there. I kept saying, mom,
can you hear me, the plane has landed,
I'll be home for dinner, but she
said nothing. I could see her face,
could see her holding the phone,
an old fashioned one, yellow coiled cord,
her head tilted, her sunny smile, but
her voice was barely discernable. I get
that she's dead, but we had a ritual—
always reported when one another landed.
My mother and I. We had a ritual.

If You See a Cobra

If you see a cobra, dial 911.
Do not touch the cobra.
Do not speak to the cobra.
Do not make eye contact
with the cobra.
Never engage with the cobra
or in any way entice the cobra,
befriend the cobra, or connect
with the cobra. If you see a cobra
pretend you're hallucinating
or imagine it's a feral cat
or a relative from the south
you thought was dead.
If you're still so unlucky
that the venomous albino
monocled snake on the loose
in Thousand Oaks bites you,
your body will go numb,
and you will start to convulse.
If not immediately treated,
you will turn into a cobra
and everyone will be looking for *you*.
Someone will spot you slithering
out of a old box. Your white color
will give you away.

Workout

I crunch my stomach
as the gym televisions blast:
interview about "Bra Balls"
women demonstrating
how you can wash your bras
worry free three at a time
keeps dainty delicates
from being crushed, twisted
even different colors won't bleed
on the other channel local woman
gets shot waiting for bus
no time to worry about her bras
worry like hunger lasts forever
I don't wear a bra close my eyes
turn up my ipod let the tunes
drench my eardrums drown out
sounds I never asked to hear
hands clasped behind my head
lift to the beat again again press
my lower back tight against the mat
stomach clenched jaw angry can't stop
thinking of the woman bleeding
on the curb even bra balls
seem more real noise blasting
gunfire for the workout lift again
again while someone else's stomach
is emptying into the gutter

LATELY HER DREAMS HAVE BEEN FILLED WITH ANIMALS

Last night she was stalked by a squirrel
his flat black eyes trailed her through long grass
in a park where she once played.

She rested on some rocks, noticed it staring
from a few feet away, not a blink, she watched it
watching her. It skidded closer, closing in,

stopped again to get a good look before lunging
at her head, digging its claws into her scalp,
and she grabbed its thick tail, hurled it down

onto the rock, suffocated it with a cotton sheet,
the soft one that used to be on her son's bed—
cowboys, horses, tumbleweed—held that squirrel

down until it shuddered into stiffness.
She awakened refreshed, no memory of her terror
until mid-morning as she walked to her car,

heard chirping, squeals, looked up at the fruit tree
to see squirrels jumping through the leaves,
a thrush of fear spreading through her body

and she clasped her hands together, squeezed
as if to gage how strong she was, what did it mean,
how could she kill a squirrel even in a dream.

My Mailman Pees on the Gate by the Dumpster

My mailman pees on the gate by the dumpster,
I've seen him do it twice. My co-worker, she's
seen him, too, was afraid to tell me for obvious
reasons, and when she told me I couldn't
believe her because it was too repulsive to picture.
But I saw him just now, again, downstairs,
I was about to throw my trash away, the end
of my workday, it's dark, and there he was,
his back facing me, arms disappearing
into the garbage bin, so I looked away fast,
scared he might turn, see me see him,
try to kill me so I wouldn't tell the police—
we've all heard the stories—
postal worker goes mad, maybe because someone
saw them peeing outside in close proximity
where they deliver the mail, and from now on
when I reach my hand into the cold metal box
it will be with trepidation, disgust, but also
sadness, imagining growing old, losing control
alone at dusk with nothing but other people's
bills and invitations stuffed into a bag, tugging
at my shoulder which burns from the weight,
fingers too stiff to unbutton the uniform I once wore
so proudly back when I didn't need to pee
with devastating urgency, when I delivered my letters
clean, immaculate, my key chain shining, dangling
engraved, "Mommy's Favorite Mailman."

SILENT LUNCH

We're all falling from the sky
like the blackbirds in Bebe:
my mother, Adrienne, Bee Gees,
the baby mountain lion
took a wrong turn so many going
and the weather's changing too
clouds thickening, swelling
as our children in school playgrounds
are condemned to silent lunches,
want to talk when they eat
have things to say why does everything
seem so sad today, I've mourned many
why does it hurt like for the first time?
I remember how my mother's mouth
hung open, how deeply asleep she was
when she passed—was she dreaming of kissing
death on the lips or of a swan circling the pond
where she tossed pennies for wishes as a girl?
Silent lunches, birds falling from the sky, music
ending, someone tell me why the schools
make our children be silent when they eat
as they sit on benches tuna salad falling
out of soft white bread smudged
by their fingers—we never had silent lunches
except sometimes I have them now
stare into my food while I swallow
remember all the people I love who've died
having silent lunches, too, crusts cut
catching bites as they float by
on a bed of clouds, scraping the bottoms
of stars for dessert.

[V]

Costume

I'm dressed as half swan, half cow:
my elegant, lethal wings grace a huge
side-cut of black and white—long ballet
neck jutting out of my thick sacred shoulder
delicate swan self meshed into the cumbersome
world of meat. Not sure about my feet,
hoofed or webbed, if I should go
tricking or treating—knocking on doors
will only confuse people.
What does a swan have to do with a cow
my friend's daughter asks me.
She doesn't understand. Feathers and bristle
lightness and bulk. I want to be in both worlds:
meander like a drunk leftover,
worshipped by angels. Plod through
grass, command the lake, be admired
for both parts of who I am.

ANOTHER BIRTHDAY

Lift off; power your way up through the fog.
Soon the haze will burn off, like the birth
of a new idea, opaque will make way for blue,
the color of your first collared shirt.
Think of all the years you've flown into,
out of, all the shirts you've unbuttoned
shoelaces you've tied. "It's just a number," we say,
who really cares—age is how we feel. We're still alive,
aren't we, even though those numbers do add up,
like birds gathering on the fence in the playground
where you flew down the slide, shrieking with childhood,
hot metal searing your sides, clueless sparrows taking off
one at a time into the cold-blooded sky where now you fly,
throttle tight in your grip, another passage, an extra high.
Celebrate because it's another way to say you're still here
and so am I, wishing you a smooth flight, though your
Mickey Mouse alarm clock ticks like a time bomb beside your bed,
remember: there's plenty of undiscovered air out there.
As you begin your descent—sleeves rolled like a 50's movie star,
cigarette pack tucked into the fold, dark glasses tight,
you may hear the sound of rain pounding the roof
like on those nights when you can't sleep, when you count
the people who've loved you. Take off or touch down
we pray the same—foreheads damp,
whispering inside our palms so no one can hear.
Breathe in, exhale, look up.
See? The air doesn't lie.

INTROSPECTION

I walk over to the full-length
mirror, take off my robe
look at my body as if I were you

looking at me, touch my breasts
drop my hand to my belly
rub and pinch as if my fingers

were yours, watch you
watch me like I'm in a play
and you're my only audience.

We're not alone.
The young girl inside me
is standing on her bed

watching her shape take form
her eyes lowered but anxious
for you to see. The pregnant me

she's here too—see how tightly
her skin is stretched
over her belly, her insides

riding her like a cannonball of waves.
Look at the scar on my left
shoulder. Have you ever noticed

that before? I need you to know
my body's whole story,
from the fever when I was born

when they lowered me
into a mixing bowl of ice
to when the bleeding began

I doubled over, no one
was there, no one can ever
really be there

can they? Even our toes change
shape in the dark.
I'm ready to be turned inside out.

4AM

silence gathers
like drifts of snow on a windowsill

she eats the quiet

not even an airplane can be heard
powering through the clouds

no one's leaving or returning
not at this private hour
when darkness is still
folded around us

she can hear a cat in the distance
close her eyes

only those asleep
are making noise
the rattle of their dreams
stirs the heavens:

nightmares are what keep
our ancestors alive

let the others sleep

she'll take a five mile run
inside her head

remember her parents
are dead

this is the time she listens

the hour she wakes
the sleeping child
in her heart

This Morning is for You

This morning is for you
sideways bird not quite awake

not ready to make
sounds that will astonish.

This morning's for you
fading stars still tucked

into the bleary sky
your final twinkle vibrating

the heavens before dawn
kills you off.

This morning is for the bruise
that lingers on my arm

purple as a groggy sunset
reminding me I can take

any punch that comes my way
silently charged as twilight

fearless as the night
fearless as I for loving you

completely as I do, surrendering
to light, black into blue,

this morning's a buried treasure
this morning is for you.

TRANSFORMATION

I gently put my finger in my eye
to remove some gunk clouding
my vision, and by mistake

I remove the eye itself.
It now sits on the tip
of my right index finger,

able to look directly at me,
me at it, able to see into
my other eye, still in place.

The lens lies flat, wrapped
around my finger, soft, flexible,
shining green iris alert, ready

black pupil like the head of a pin.
From its new perspective
my eye can really look out for me,

see things I've not be able
to see, watch me watch myself
without using a mirror.

The eye on my finger has begun
to point me in another direction,
lead me through the 200 million mile

tunnel to the other side
of longing, help me see I no longer
need you. The eye in my face

may be gone but what remains is not
an empty socket, but a place to store
memories so a new eye can form.

Ode to OCD

Praise paperclips!
How they must be moved
each hour, red ones
to the left
pink in a middle pile
green and blue
can never touch
for life to go on.
Praise her egg shaped
carnival glass
paper weight!
Watch how she cradles it
in her palm
strokes it twice
delicious numbers
2, 4, 6, 8, 10
nails that tap
repeated mantras
obsessive longing
his mouth his chin his mouth
his chin, what if he doesn't,
what if he's in, I promise to
I promise to I never will
I never do.
Praise fallen eyelashes
to flick for a wish
floors that can be scrubbed
again
and again
red glass strawberry

in her pocket
keeps her calm
so life can go on.
Praise anxiety,
that ultramarine speedboat
racing through her brain.
Isn't it the motor
that's kept her running?
Is it not the child
she gave birth to
on the day she was born?

You Remind Me I Long for the Clouds

you remind me I long for the clouds
though you cannot promise
they won't explode

you tell me to embrace
the love that burns through me
hot as August sun

terrifying as the music of hands
of years as I fly home
above the storm birds

rolling on the wings
calling your name
reminding me I long for quiet

the kind we won't even have
in death the white sound
inside our kiss

silence of air
before thunder begins before
the plane glides under

the final layer of clouds
as it touches down
soon your embrace

"DYING IS NOT BLACK,"

Erica tells me,
from her dying mother's
bedside, her mother
who still rejoices
in her daughter's colors
reaches out to touch
as did mine
at the very end
her eyes gray
blue
turning
green
the color
I feared.
"I love that color on you,"
my mother said
the night she died,
reaching her shaky hand
to touch the pink
of my scarf. *"I prefer
earth tones, you know,
for myself, that is,
but on you . . .*
and off she drifted
an evening shadow
fading into shallow
breathing
as I closed
her blue eyes
for the first time.

My Guardian

Lolita, Karen's black and white spotted dog
slept in bed with me last night.
I'm a houseguest,
and Lolita, Lola for short, jumped high onto the bed

where she's never allowed to be, covering the quilt,
that covered me in the dark Portland room.
I opened my eyes, there she was, her nose pointed

at mine and half awake I thought I was a dog, too,
part of her pack, her daughter or sister from another litter.
I hunched into a ball
so we could be the same shape, together

in our den, was honored that Lola chose to sleep next to me.
Karen's other dogs, gorgeous Great Pyrenees, *not herders*
but guardians, were holed-up with Karen, while Lola, a mutt,
was looking out for *me*

as cool fall breezes shimmied
through the cracks of the window, leaves on the trees
turned orange through the night, as a trail of dusty

clouds obscured the traveling moon, we slept
our dreams spilling over
into the other

Lola entered a long room, humans dressed
in evening clothes, their tall backs against the wall, offering
her pearls and steak, while I was locked

inside a crate,
my paw stuck in the black wires, my tongue hanging out, hoping
for the sort of kindness an animal may find.

Cat without a Name

A lean black cat visits my back yard:
long, sleek, silver tags clicking,
one that says, "I am an outside cat,"
the other, "I know my way home."

Who are you, little cat, I ask him,
why is there no name on your tag?
"The Good the Bad and the Ugly" of cats,
he's Clint Eastwood's character reincarnated

a kindred spirit, no name cat, in one yard
out the other, killing any rats, squirrels
in his path. I reach out with shredded cheddar
but no name cat refuses. I present him

a cup of cream, a pinch of sliced turkey,
offer a fingertip of yogurt,
but no name cat just wants to be stroked
as he purrs while listening for sounds

whistling through my avocado tree,
birds colliding with the wind, morning sky
milky white, June gloom, black cat here
to make sure everything's ok, as he places

his paw on my leg, like he's blessing me
before leaving for another town, moving on
to a better yard, perhaps one with lemon grass,
lilies, fat lizards, richer road kill.

REACHING FOR THE MOON

Tonight the moon will be so close
you can climb a tree, the tips
of your fingers will almost touch
its marbled face. Try to kiss
its luminescence as it floods you
with desire, anticipation consuming
your body as you swoon deeper
into yourself, a cat in heat craving
what is not beautiful. Stretch
for your moon, bigger than you've ever
imagined. You can no longer ignore
what compels you to reach for sadness.
Longing is what lifts you; only a lifetime
of sorrow will fill you with joy.

The Truth about Wishes

Each day before dawn
I take my wish for a walk
We begin our journey
Together in the dark

Hike up the mountain
As the sky turns light
My wish in my pocket
Has slept through the night

Each day after lunch
I take my wish for a drive
We roll down the windows
We both feel alive

Right before sleep
I put my wish in my hair
My wish becomes frantic
It's easy to scare

They never told me
I never knew
Only if you abandon your wish
Will it ever come true

Yet an unmade wish
Is constantly on fire
It searches for purpose
It's the heat of desire

[VI]

For Emily on Her Birthday

You could wade grief,
Whole pools of it
You were used to that
But the least push of joy
Would make you dizzy.

I understand. Happy birthday,
Now and every year after
Think of us together
Sipping from that generous pool
Swallowing tears by the mouthful

As we carefully bat stars
From our eyes, afraid to catch
Light, even for a moment.
I would have lived no better in your time
Than you would live now in mine.

The hectic pace of compliments,
Rejection—the water we splash
Onto our faces and the faces of those
Who do not love us, have never loved us,
Even the ones who loved us true

Oh, Emily, we've learned from you
Of solitude and introspection
Building memories of our own invention
What are we supposed to do
Alone in our thoughts without you?

A Woman Driving a Hearse Dies While Driving

A woman driving a hearse dies while driving.
They find her slumped over her steering wheel
en route to a funeral. Police cannot immediately say
to what cemetery the now dead woman was driving
the already dead woman. I once drove my dead cat
into the woods because burying a cat in the city is just
not right. What if I had died on the way—was found
slumped over the steering wheel of my Infiniti?
Would anyone have discovered my dead cat packed
in the Italian shoe box in the trunk?
(where are those shoes now?)
The hearse driver, they say, died of natural causes,
but what's natural about driving a dead person
you don't even know to a funeral?
Did this hearse driver plan her own death, distressed
she drove a hearse, jealous of the dead she drove,
sick of wondering what it's like to be dead?
We'll never know. Dead people can't talk.
Not the same, however, for cats, and my cat
won't shut up. I hear her in my sleep, perpetually
in heat, stepping over stars like dead bodies,
clawing her way to the moon.

MY MOTHER BAKES SUGAR COOKIES

My mother bakes sugar cookies
in Heaven which is funny
because she never baked
here on earth.

They have you doing that
first thing, she told me

They have you baking
right away so you'll feel useful
we deliver the cookies
to children who've passed

The people in charge of Heaven
sound so thoughtful, I tell her.
Well, they're angels,
she says,

but not like you'd imagine.
Sure, they wear white,
have wings,
smile sweetly

but they all talk way too much,
and their asses
are huge.

Woman in Auditorium Nods Her Head

Sitting in a packed auditorium,
listening to a lecture on the brain,
the woman in front of me
nods her head
to everything that's being said.
No matter what he says
her head bobs yes yes yes
moving so fast it looks from the back
as if she's having an epileptic fit: Yes!
Yes! Yes! Yes! Yes! she nods
at every remark he makes
sentences he barely finishes,
thoughts he only begins to develop,
there she goes—she's nodding, nodding
yes yes yes yes yes before his thought is even
articulated she's right with him, she knows what he's about to say,
can *feel* the words about to topple out
drop from his brain to his mind, out through his mouth,
like waiting for her luggage on a conveyor belt she's poised
to grab that bag, knows just what's in it,
nodding at everything, things I hardly comprehend
she's right there—*cerebrum, cerebellum, central nervous system,*
nod nod nod nod nodding quick fast jerky nods like we do
when someone's talking to us way too fast
and we're trying to keep up with their words, keep rhythm
brain stem controls vital body functions . . . her nods trail off,
slow down, the way we nod when our child tries to explain
where it hurts we encourage them to describe
the exact place, slowly nodding looking into their eyes
tell all, tell mommy everything, or when a lover tells us

there's someone new, nod, nod, slower, yes, yes, again please,
a slanted kind of nod, an I see nod and there she goes, shifting nods
once more, impatient nod, the nod that says, I know, I know, I know, I know
what you're saying, finish your thought, get it over with, oh, please stop
all the nods are happening at once, a repertoire of nods
a plethora of nods, a dance of nods, nod fusion, theatre of nods, I'm dizzy
watching the back of her head go up and down, trying to imagine
what she understands and agrees with so completely, imagining
her brain cramped with yeses slithering around her hypothalamus,
her body turning hot and cold through restless nights
of unquenchable desire to accept the impossible.

Abandoned

They were in the gutter
a pair of man-sized
flip flops, fat toe prints embedded
in the rubber, not really old
still looked in decent shape
but some man kicked them off
discarded them, left them
to get rolled over by a stroller
run over by a Toyota or bus load
of children eating Cheese-Its
texting pictures of naked body parts
final assault to a pair of innocent flip
flops. Who would do such a thing?
What kind of man
wears flip flops
tosses them into the street
when he no longer wants them?
Is he the kind of man you'd respect?
Want? Could you love this man?
I do. I love him for walking barefoot
down Genessee, the heat of asphalt
searing his calloused feet. I love him
for wanting to be free of silly shoes
that offer no support, no elegance, shoes
to put on in a hurry, without thought
shoes that make a slapping smacking sound
shoes you want to happily abandon knowing
a stranger is likely to step on them
crush their uselessness.
I love him for ending it.

While Waiting on the Food Truck Line

"I could see you having like an awesome
bald head," one girl says to another
waiting on line for Indian food.

I'm dying for curried potatoes and chicken
in a taco, deep fried, served with mango
salsa, but this is killing my appetite.

I can't see their faces, but from the back
they have a ton of hair, colorful mermaid
tattooed on the dark one's shoulder

the blonde has a mole at the nape of her neck.
"You're cute enough, she goes on, it'd be ok,
but what would your boyfriend say?"

I wonder would I ever shave my head?
I imagine living in a village of bald people,
in a room with only a razor, straight pin, alcohol

swabs, lime-scented shaving cream,
pink and yellow flamingos painted on the ceiling,
listen to hair disappear from heads drenched

in light, hairless angels with pierced wings feeding me
while telling stories of hairless ghosts, a voice
interrupting, "are you ready to order?"

GOOD LUCK

It's good luck to leave
money on the floor
one guy said to the other.
Counter of Jan's on Beverly.
So on the way out
I nonchalantly drop a five
on checkered linoleum.
I need good luck.
Maybe when I return home
there were be a fountain
in my living room
brimming with gold coins,
three genies waiting in the kitchen,
a prince sipping compari
in my back yard,
purple flowers bursting
out of the earth around him.
Maybe my life, that has been drained
of meaning, will fill up with reasons;
I will see everything in a new light:
sunset, the bruise sinking into the ocean
will become a luscious ball of fire
exploding into the sea.
The moon, a cold warning hanging
onto the metal sky
will become my guide, the promise
pulling me back into myself.
The man at Jan's digging his fingers
into his lint filled pockets
doesn't know the genie is already

in his home, tearing through drawers
trying on his pajamas, stretching his
worn out wishes, turning them inside out.

FRIENDS DON'T LET FRIENDS PLEAD GUILTY

Friends don't let friends jump into lakes
filled with glass, polish their toenails
flat black tie their shoe laces into knots.
Friends don't let friends eat two day old sushi,
marry people with no friends, soak in tubs
stained with blood, cry over an old lover,
tell the same story more than once unless
they're telling it to new friends. Friends
don't let friends wear neck ties with pictures of
cartoon characters, call one another bi-polar, take
long walks in the dark by a river no one swims in
near a train station no one stops at in a town
no one's heard of unless they take their dog.

HERE'S YOUR TITLE

Make one up. This poem will surely need one.
Call it Blue: like the way children paint the sky,
the sky that's never really blue. Call it Yellow:
the color of lemons on the tree outside my window,
though those are smudged with black soot, never ripe
enough, but we squeeze their juice anyway.
Call the poem Red: color of blood, though blood is more
rust or burgundy, not the red of my grandmother's lipstick
smeared over her white teeth that were never really white.
Forget calling it a color at all, because already we see colors
mean different things to different people, not specific enough
for a poem title. Call it Disillusionment, a poem about the way
we wish things were, or might be, like we wish the lemons
were sweeter, or the sky *really* blue, or how when I walked
to the corner I wish I hadn't seen a man sleeping on the sidewalk,
wrapped in a blanket of stars. I looked quickly, then up at the sky
filled with clouds, birds like black marks crossing out the white.
I cannot feel the air. It's too still to name. Are you really the way
you appear? Come here. Do you trust me to hold your face
in my hands? Make your ending stronger than your title. Do it.
Do it fast before your choices attack you one by one.

"Would you donate your brain to science?"

the stranger in the linen department of Macy's
asks me? I look around to be sure she's talking
to me. "I don't know, would you?" I reply,
not knowing what else to say, what really can
one say? Maybe this person has already
donated her brain to science and that's why
she's asking me this question. "I'm thinking
about it," she says, "I wish I could donate it
while I'm still alive so they could tell me why
I need to move objects around on my desk,
why I can never settle on the perfect shade of red,
why I can't accept love." "I have a brain," I tell her,
"and I'm holding onto it." I want to see if it will
deteriorate on its own, organically like my mother's,
leaving me unabashedly knowing what I want:
no excuses, denial, shame, debate, just silence,
shh, a moment to feel the thrill of only what I need:
tissues, a breeze, macaroni and cheese.
At last I will be the perfect gift to myself.

Do Not Disturb

"I could sleep for days on a bed of lapels,"
my friend Debra says.
I understand. I could sleep for days
on a couch of buttonholes.
We're tired.
Everyone's tired.
My dog has been sleeping
in a bed of dog hair all afternoon.
I don't know why
he's so tired; all he does is sleep,
but I'm trying not to judge.
I now believe sleeping
is as important as being awake,
that we make our clearest decisions
in the bleary gray moments
of eyelid flutter, lifting our heavy legs
in and out of the warm stream of dreams
where sheep and cows float like barges through clouds,
stray bullets catch breezes as we hold hands
jump through windows wave goodbye to our dead
loved ones who are wearing clothing we thought
we'd discarded.
Let's go to sleep now.
Come here.
Lie down beside me.
It's our time to rest.
Put on my golden pajamas,
satin blindfold scented with lavender.
It's too late for us to be awakened
by the trivial needs of others.
I'm drowsy with expectations.

[VII]

No Resolution

New Year's Eve and once more
they are here, stepping in time
to music from their parent's world:

Martin, Sinatra, Day, mouthing words
not meant for them. She thinks
each dance will be their last

until the drinking begins—
rose hips and vodka, taking her far away
to a world of tongues, lips

crashing waves . . . *Baby it's cold outside,*
I've got to go away, I really can't stay . . .
music of infidelity carrying her through,

just enough of a beat to stay in a lie.
Baby it's bad out there; Say, what's in this drink?
Routine wraps around her

like burlap drapes too heavy to hang
she struggles to cut away
as she braces herself to begin the new year

forcing herself to believe it's all meant to be,
while inside her bedside drawer
her golden scissors sparkle.

THROWING OUT THE FLOWERS

I used to hate throwing out the flowers
tossing the dead when only a week ago
they were lush, vibrant, stamens intact
their greenness staining my fingers,
fragrance so potent I had to hold at arm's length.
Now, thick, bloated with yesterday, their crusted petals
are chips of fading color dropping on my glass table top.
I used to hate them for dying; feel sorry for myself
having to pull them out of the vase, careful not to
inhale their rancid remains, carry them dripping
across the kitchen to the green can and say goodbye:
I remember seeing you at the Farmer's Market,
so fresh, colorful, calling me to take you home.
Now look at you!
But, today I'm okay. Content to move on knowing
there are plenty of fresh flowers in my future,
many stiffer stems to bring home, clip.
Listen for the music of flowers dying.

What Are the Nuns Doing That
They Can't Answer the Phone?

Are they praying so loudly even their silent
desire drowns out the rings?
They are releasing blessings to their Lord
as if blowing air into a tender balloon,
colorless as wishes they will never touch.
The nuns are praying for us,

praying we'll escape the flames,
be forgiven for what we can't name,
as they pluck weeds from gardens unknown,
eat from food trucks driven by angels,
tie shoes from another century,
they are singing *His* songs, for us, paving a road
to the heart of God whom they love like a rock star,
preparing for the day they'll meet—
run off together into the windy white light,
a flock of soaring nuns with their golden God.

I wanted to be a nun when I was six,
saw one in a movie, she healed a child with her touch,
her silky coif, a sacred ballerina in simple black flats,
giant pockets filled with light.
I wanted to wear her veil, pray to God, too,
but didn't know what to say.
Should I whisper? Ask for a sacred stone,
promise to be good forever?

What are the nuns doing that they can't answer the phone,
the Pope asked when he called the Carmelites

on New Year's Eve?
Shouldn't he know?

They're fertilizing the world with the presence of God,
their soft hands folded inside habits
damp with spirituality.

Nuns entrenched in praying for us,
because they must—*as if*
they don't have a life. As if
they need to wait by the phone.

WHY I'M TOO TIRED TO DO ANYTHING

I just read a book about the Pilgrims

I went on a five mile run inside my own head

My children accused me of stealing coins from their pockets

My husband accused me of starving the goldfish

My dog appears to be listless

I found a letter my mother sent me in high school

I just remembered my father is dead

I'm trying to understand why girls obsess over horses

Last night I wandered into someone else's dream

I cleaned out a drawer and found a sweater belonging to you

Why We Dream

My mother has been dead for 10 months
but last night I dreamed she was alive
and we met somewhere in L.A., nowhere
I'd ever been before, it was hilly more
like San Francisco, clear air everywhere,
and she had long, straight, thick red hair,
nothing like her no hair before she died.
She was wearing my black cashmere coat,
too big for me so I gave it to my aunt
in real life, one Fall trip back to New York.
When I told my mother that I gave it to my aunt
she was mad then happy because it made me
a nice person and proved she'd been a good mother.
I said in my dream, *mom, you look so young,
so new*—her evening gloves chic sliding under
the softness of the coat, her beret slanted
just so, her 40's movie star smile, lots of teeth,
dimples, lipstick and charm—I'm not dead,
she said, *I'm going to the Opera!* This is the kind
of dream that helps me live with the nightmares.

My Dog Walks Out

My dog walks out
of the bedroom
realizes there's nothing

for him
living room lonely
no food on the floor

no clouds in the sky
he looks up
as if birds might fly

over the couch
onto the book shelf
but there are none

he walks back
into the bedroom
finds my discarded

sweater with traces
of me for him
presses his dog chin

into the softness
dreams of the way
things will never be

In Search of a Sidekick

Female looking for a sidekick,
woman, if possible, who'll worship me
and always be by my side, (which goes
without saying). You must laugh at my jokes
but not in a fake way, run out for snacks,
protect me from dogs, pretend I'm somebody special,
walk ahead of me, point me out and say, *have you met her,*
she's so great, you should know her, but you'll never confess,
no, not to anyone you're my sidekick, not even when tortured.
We wouldn't have to ride on horses like on old television
shows, (Zorro and Bernardo), and there are no capes
or costumes involved. If you are looking for a great opportunity,
(without pay), and a way to make someone
feel special, please write to PO Box 666. I promise you
a chance to completely forget who you are.

A Fly with One Wing Is Watching Me

I remember this fly from long ago
when it had two wings. I was living
in Boston, tried to kill it so many hot
summer nights, terrorized me as I
tried to sleep, circling the chaos
in my head, knew him so well
I called him Jack, tried to make it
a fun thing, this fly intent on ruining
my life. Now he's in L.A., languishing
on the soft chair across the room,
watching me work. I can see he's less
a fly since he's lost a wing, and I want
to know his anguish. *Come here little fly,*
I gently call to him, but flies are so
nervous, they think we're all trying
to kill them so they don't wait to hear
what we have to say. I approach him
slowly, put my finger out, invite him
to hop on but he doesn't move. Maybe
his one wing is too tired to lift, so I sit
next to him, remind him of his glory
days back when he could torment me
how much fun it must have been for him.
He doesn't move. I consider flicking him
across the room or smashing him
right there, but why? It's clear he came by
to see me, find out how I'm doing,
acknowledge the past when his buzz
was his life and he couldn't resist
being the best fly he could be.

LIPSTICK READING

I had my lipstick read at a cocktail party,
had to apply then kiss a glossy index card
as if it was the love of my life.
I kissed the slick paper open-mouthed;
the imprint of my lips like a song.
My lipstick color is "Heroine,"
purple with an undercurrent of blush,
a hue that shows no remorse.
Even the reader is fooled:
thinks I'm an impulsive romantic, willing
to fly to Paris on a whim—you'll try anything
he told me—because your lips are parted,
yet, the corners are joined together:
A circle of friends, holding hands, white sky
in the middle, a hole for me to disappear into.
Just tell me, I ask, tell me about the crease
on my upper lip. Read it. Explain why
it's always been there; a trail leading nowhere.

Candlelight Asylum

Do not enter my candlelight asylum
where we dance in our terry cloth robes,
hair pinned up like discarded Barbies,
our feet crushed in pink ballet slippers.
I lied.
There is no one here.
I am all alone, just me
in my grown up sled bed, comforter
around my feet, head propped with flat pillows,
no cases, yellow around the edges,
a furnace coughing up wet music.
This is no place for someone so alive, juicy
abundantly humane,
so soft in her silk underwear.
You may enter, but
only you, you with the smile and dark hair,
you with the stride, the hands.
You look like you could get me
out, and I trust that you will.
Come on in.
No one here but me
and the candles, though they're burning fast,
room darkening as the breeze pours through the windows.
I don't even know your name or where you're from.
Please take my slippers.
No one is listening
my inside voice, my inside words, no one hears—
not even the handsome nurse
who brings my tray of kisses.
Oh I lied again, there is no nurse.

Don't believe a word I tell you, but please
take me away.
Do I have to wait for disaster before someone
plucks me
like the wilted daisy in the jar by the window,
places me in clear water in a silver vase? Hurry
before sunset goes bad. Join me
on the last train to the missing planet.

BIOGRAPHICAL NOTE

Kim (Freilich) Dower was born and raised in New York City and received a BFA in Creative Writing from Emerson College, where she also taught creative writing. Her first collection of poetry, *Air Kissing on Mars*, (Red Hen Press, 2010) was on the Poetry Foundation's Contemporary Best Sellers list, and was described by the *Los Angeles Times* as, "sensual and evocative . . . seamlessly combining humor and heartache." *Slice of Moon*, her second collection (Red Hen Press, 2013), nominated for a Pushcart, was called, "unexpected and sublime," by *O Magazine*. Kim's work has been featured in Garrison Keillor's, "The Writer's Almanac," and Ted Kooser's, "American Life in Poetry," as well as in *Barrow Street, Eclipse, Los Angeles Review, Ploughshares*, and *Rattle*. Her poems are included in the anthology, *Wide Awake: Poets of Los Angeles and Beyond*, published by The Pacific Coast Poetry Series, an imprint of Beyond Baroque Books. She teaches a workshop called, *Poetry and Dreaming* in the B.A. Program of Antioch University and she lives in West Hollywood, California. To learn more about Kim, visit www.kimdowerpoetry.com.